The Christmas Bird

by Sallie Ketcham

Illustrations by
Stacey Schuett

THE CHRISTMAS BIRD

Cover and book design by Michelle L. Norstad

ISBN 0-8066-3871-0

The paper used in this publication meets the minimum requirements of American National Standard for Information Sciences—Permanence of Paper for Printed Library Materials, ANSI Z329.48-1984. ♾ ™

Manufactured in the U.S.A.   AF 9-3871

04   03   02   01   00   1   2   3   4   5   6   7   8   9   10

To my mother, Sally Johnson Ketcham, who keeps Christmas well all the year.
    —S.K.

To Clare and Ian.
    —S.S.

Weary and wing-sore, the little bird hovered over the tiny village in Palestine. Touched by the quiet moon, her shadow dropped over the inn.

"If I knew the way south like other birds," she said to herself as she always did on the coldest nights of the year, "I would winter in Paradise."

Hugging her wings to her drab brown breast, she hopped into the stable and chirped a greeting to the cow who shared her home. She cocked a black eye at the hard dirt floor where sometimes she found bits of grain amid the chaff.

"Hush, my friend," lowed the old brown cow, "the babe's asleep."

Startled, the bird flew up and landed on the cow's bony shoulder. "Why, there is a child in the manger," she whispered, confused. "Whatever is happening?"

"Something special, I think," murmured the cow.

The child's mother inched closer to the flickering fire her husband had built. Her blue hood tumbled from her shiny black hair. She raised herself on one elbow and looked at the baby. "It is a beautiful night to be born," she said.

"It is a terrible night to be born," thought the bird, ignoring millions of brilliant stars cartwheeling over the sky. "It is cold, and I cannot warm myself."

"Ah," said the cow, "more visitors."

Two young boys and their father stumbled into the stable and pressed themselves against the far wall. They leaned heavily on their staves, breathing hard from a long run through the frosty air.

Silently the older shepherd removed his cloak and offered it to the young woman's husband, who draped it gently over his wife.

Eyeing the small fire, the bird hopped toward the manger. "It is too cold for the child," she chirped nervously.

Even as she said it, the baby stirred in the straw. The bird crept toward the fire circle and peered at the embers. Lacking fuel, tiny bits of fire struggled in the sooty ashes.

The bird moved closer to the flames until she felt
the fire at her feet. She began to beat her wings,
slowly at first, then faster, until the sparks blazed
into flame. Her tired wings began to throb, but she
beat them even harder until the flames rose high,
throwing long shadows on the walls.

Without a word, the shepherds began to break their
staves and cast the pieces on the fire.

Soon the wood kindled, and the flames bathed the family in red-gold light. There was no sound but for the breathing of the baby and the steady *whooshing* of the bird's wings. The little bird turned her head from the blast of heat and fanned the flames until they crackled and roared with warmth.

At last satisfied and exhausted, she lurched away and settled on the side of the manger.

The bird stared down at her breast in amazement. "Why, I've singed myself," she said. Her plain brown feathers were deep red, as red as any pomegranate.

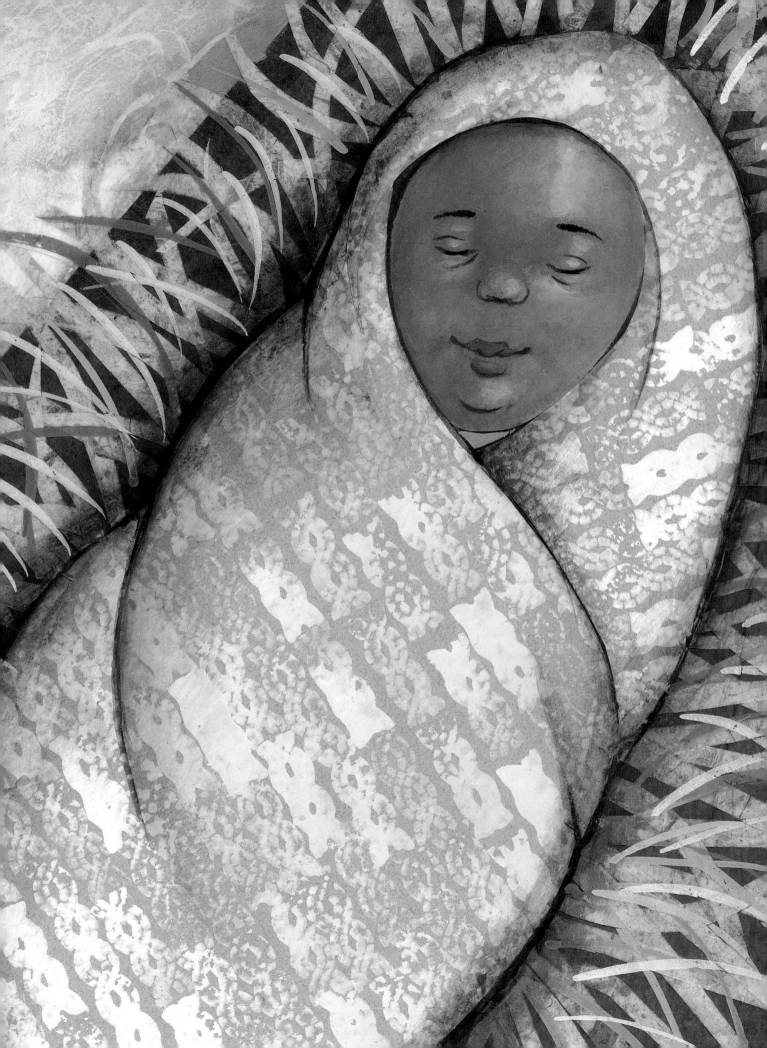

"Little bird," the young mother called softly, extending her hand. "Come, Robin."

Flying to the outstretched hand, the bird thought, "She knows my name. How does she know my name?"

"Kind Robin," the young woman whispered, stroking the bird's bright feathers, "when you fly away, keep the morning sun over your brave left wing."

"I will remember," the bird chirped.

"I will remember you, Robin, and keep you in my heart."

The little bird left at dawn, flying south over the brown hills of Palestine, with the winter sun rising on her left wing.

In time, her red-breasted children and her children's children scattered throughout the world. Before they left, she shared with them the story of their bright red feathers, and the secret of flying by the sun.

Even today the robin's children soar south in winter. But they all return home to herald the first cold days of spring, and beat their strong, small wings and flash their fine, red feathers like fire in the snow.

For Taylor, the best Christmas gift ever.

Also Illustrated by Janie Bynum:

ROCK-A-BABY BAND

BATHTUB BLUES

PORCUPINING

Little, Brown and Company

Time Warner Book Group
1271 Avenue of the Americas, New York, NY 10020
Visit our Web site at www.lb-kids.com

First Edition: October 2005

Library of Congress Cataloging-in-Publication Data

Bynum, Janie.
  Santa Baby / adapted and illustrated by Janie Bynum.-- 1st ed.
    p. cm.
  Text adapted from the lyrics of the original "Santa Baby" song composed by Joan Javi
      Phil Springer and Tony Springer.
  Summary: In this adaptation of the Christmas song "Santa Baby," a child dressed as Santa helps his mother as she decorates the tree, ties bows on gifts, and rolls out dough for holiday baking.
  ISBN 0-316-00067-1
  1. Children's songs--United States--Texts. [1. Christmas--Songs and music. 2. Songs.] I. Tit
PZ8.3.B9935San 2005
782.42164'0268--dc22

                                                    2004023

10 9 8 7 6 5 4 3 2 1

TWP

Book design by Tracy Shaw

Printed in Singapore

The illustrations for this book were done in watercolor and mixed media.
The text was set in Twinkle, and the display type is Blackfriar.

Santa
Baby

Adapted and Illustrated by

Janie Bynum

LITTLE, BROWN AND COMPANY
New York ❧ Boston

Santa Baby,
creeping, crawling under the tree.
Oh, whee!
So many things to explore.

Santa Baby,
let's snuggle close and cuddle tonight.

Santa Baby,
   help me make this ribbon a bow.
      You know
we have more presents to wrap.
      Santa Baby,
let's snuggle close and cuddle tonight.

Santa Baby,
all those tempting ornaments glow.
Uh-oh!

We'll place those high on the tree.
Santa Baby,
let's snuggle close and cuddle tonight.

Look outside. The sky is white!
A million tiny snowflakes sparkle,
diamond-bright.
So many things to see and do,
this Christmas Eve, just me and you.

Santa Baby,
rolling out the cinnamon dough.

Just so.

We'll save a few for the pan.
Santa Baby,
let's snuggle close and cuddle tonight.

Santa Baby,
hang those pretty stockings with care,
right there.

Can't wait to see what we get.
Santa Baby,
let's snuggle close and cuddle tonight.

Santa Baby,
watching tree lights glitter and glow,
let's go.

Looks like it's past your bedtime.

Santa Baby,
let's snuggle close and cuddle tonight.

Twinkling eyes and cheeks so rosy.
Snuggle into bed and I'll wrap you up cozy.

Shhh. Listen, are those hoofbeats I hear?

Has someone landed on our roof with flying reindeer?

Santa Baby,
you know you should be dreaming by now.
Oh, wow!
I hear sleigh bells outside.

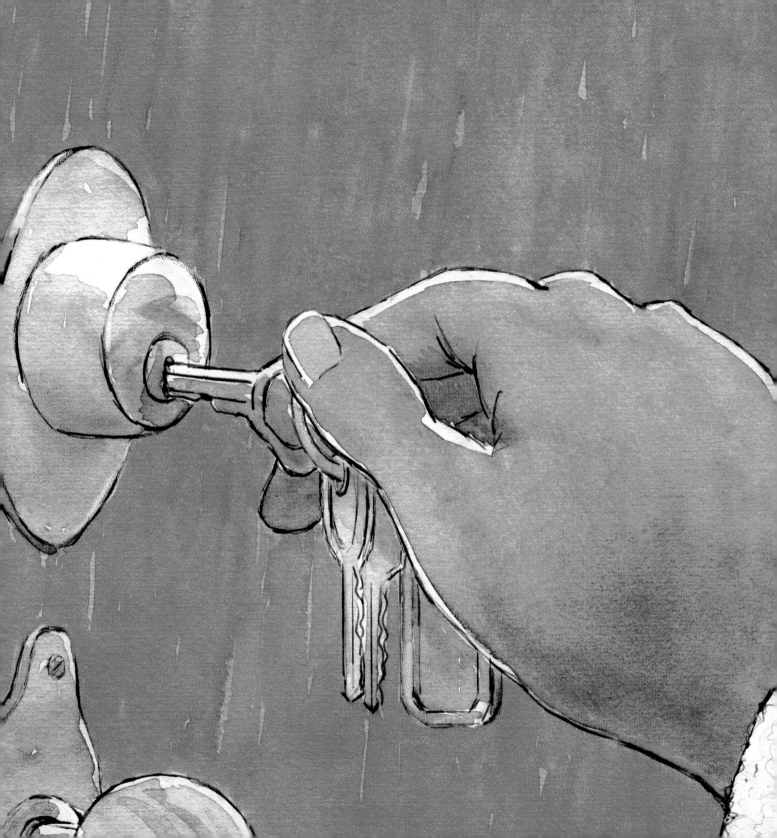

Santa Baby,
let's snuggle close and cuddle tonight.